I0529972

Small Gestures

poetry by

Melissa Wray

Copyright 2024, Melissa Wray.
Author's preferred edition
Published by Grand River Poetry Collective.
ISBN: 978-1-968226-01-5
The works herein may only be quoted or published
with permission of Melissa Wray

Acknowledgements
Thank you to graybeard courage-teacher Dave Cope, and to Sue
Cope,
for their continuous encouragement.

Publication Information
Some of these poems have appeared in *Big Scream*, *Big Hammer*,
Napalm Health Spa, *Display* and *Voices*.

Cover
Design by Don Mangione
Sparrow painting by Amy Armstrong

Grand River Poetry Collective
https://grandriverpoetrycollective.com

For my mother, Ninfa Russo; thank you
for teaching me resilience and compassion.

Contents

First Set: Small Gestures

Second Set: New Pictures

Third Set: Iris

First Set: Small Gestures

Bus Stop

A stately old black man
holds a plastic sack
containing a porn magazine
and the biggest jug
of Hawaiian Punch
I've ever seen:
the land of milk
and honey.

Pink spaghetti straps

and blond hair
skimming
sharp shoulder blades
frail arms
and slim wrists
resting small hands
on narrow hips
short dress
barely covering
tight
slightly spread
thighs
standing
in front
of a gas station
on the corner
of Wealthy
and Division—
he
was beautiful.

City Music

A homeless man walking
with a sack full
of clanging glass bottles,
squealing brakes,
neighbors shouting greetings
from dark porches—
a drunk leaving a liquor store
scat sings
in a concrete parking lot.

Blues

A man
is singing
the blues—
rudimentary rhymes
drawling languidly
the sounds dribbling from his lips
slippery
splatting stains
on his lapel
like spilled bourbon.

Hotel

She's slumped
on the hard bench
squeezing
her red feet
into stockings
tying
a white apron
around her
black-clothed waist
pulling on
thick-soled shoes
and yelling in Vietnamese
back and forth
across the locker room
to other women
in the same ritual—
her last
exhalations
before
dragging
her cleaning cart
through suites.

He Makes His Way

He makes his way slowly
dragging one leg
one arm raised at the elbow
his hand a frozen claw
ribbons of thick drool
stringing
from his always open mouth:
stuck strained yellow grin.
He approaches two small children
and softly pats them on the head.
Their mother smiles
and nods at him
as the children cling to her
with wide
scared
curious
eyes.

Averting Eyes

A beautiful young woman
white shirt
caramel skin
steps slowly onto the bus,
wades through greedy
startled
averting eyes,
sinks into her seat,
passes a small
blood-caked hand
over scratches
on her chest and cheek
for a place to rest her forehead.
People shift
off
on—
she pulls the string,
gathers a folder,
a box of crayons,
silently leaves.

Home

I am walking home
in the dark
rounding a familiar corner.
"Hey precious,
thanks for the cigarette,"
she says, and
"you better walk faster
in this neighborhood."
I saw her
days before
in a seedy market
buying Faygo pop
with the last dollar
on her Bridge card.
She left that night
as I was lighting up
in the parking lot.
"Can I buy a cigarette from you?
How much you want,
a quarter?"
I gave her one
without the quarter.
"Oh, thank you!
I'll go home and
have my dinner
and a smoke.
Thank you!"
She remembered me
and thanked me again.

I continue walking.
A man in front of me

on the sidewalk
is pulling up
scratching
guttural sounds
from deep in his gut
in rhythm
with his step,
he turns slightly
and eyes me,
I try to pass him.
He taps me on the shoulder.
I continue walking.
He taps me on the shoulder
silently
unfolds a piece of paper
may I have $1.00
for foods?
I reach into my pocket
and hand him one.
He thanks me
in sign language
then pulls me in
for a hug.

Coma

He asks me for a cigarette,
I give him a djarum.
"It's not quite a cigarette,"
I tell him.

"Anything'll do,"
he answers,
"How old are you?"

"Twenty-three."

He leans against
the bus stop pole,
pulling down his collar
to show a vicious
red scar
across his throat—
"I was in a coma when I was nineteen;
twenty-four days"—
he lifts his sweater
to expose
another scar
raised and winding
marring
his pale hairy belly.
"Hit by a drunk driver—
I woke up,
lost sixty-three pounds
in twenty-four days."

"Must change
your perspective on things."

"Yeah—
I still drink
but I don't drink and drive.
Do you have a boyfriend?"

"Yes."

He leans his head back,
blatantly disappointed,
sits on the bench
and starts talking
to the girl
next to me.

Meat

An old black man on the trolley
with a bucket of roses
singing songs
he thought he knew
his nicotine-yellow hands
raised and shaking with words
about demons and devils
god's children
and his son's huge cock,
kept eyeing me
as a boy with a guitar
laughed
and eyed me
from the other side.

BABY GIRL

Around the corner
is the men's building:
Project Rehab.
I walk past several times a day
and it's the same
every time:

"Baby girl!
HEY! BABY GIRL!"
"What's your name,
sexy?"
"Wish I was walking with you."
"Can I get your phone number?"
Near him, there's one who always
hisses
at me
through his teeth:

Their faces
torsos
hang from the buildings'
high windows
screaming
for a piece.

Are they
desperate
caged
men,
or just the
regular
kind?

Slither

They slithered
up the sidewalk.
One was tall,
his bones covered by a hat
a red bandanna
and a tattered
open
dark coat
exposing a brown-bagged
pint of whiskey
shoved
under the belt
holding up his sagging jeans.
"Hello,
young lady,"
he said brightly
arms open
palms forward
fingers wiggling—
men on both sides
brushing
my ass
as they parted
and I
passed through.

Pretty Girls

I purge
on the page
because
pretty girls
don't
walk alone,
shit,
or drink
whiskey.

Panic

Body spasming
secluded
in an inclined hospital bed
sucking for breath
through an oxygen mask,
selfishly,
I wanted him there
clutching my numbing hands
as the nurse sedated me with a needle.

After, I became
grateful
he was spared.

Modesty

There has to be
a sitter
in my hospital room
at all times.
I have to
piss
with the bathroom door
open.
Fuck it.
I want them to see me
draining diarrhea
or changing my tampon.
They've seen me
blacked out
incoherent
violently vomiting acrid green-black bile
retching on nothing left
cold sweating
numb tingling blind
after teeth-clenching phobic IV changes
and blood-letting needle stings.
I want to leave
the back of my gown
half-open
when it's a boy
sitting there.
I want to receive
a visitor
and tongue and grope
until we are wildly fucking in my adjustable bed

sending pleasure moans ringing through the sterile germ halls
instead of pain.

We are all uncomfortable.

Sobriety at last

I SMELL LIKE ASS.
STERILE IS FILTHY.
LET ME OUT.
NO MORE GODDAMN INSTANT MASHED POTATOES.
I'M NOT DEAD.

Grand Entrance

Hospital protocol—
I was feeling clear-headed
optimistic
yet brought to the next institution
in a stretcher,
propped up carefully
wrapped in white cloth
rolling above everyone
bracelet on my arm
blue blood apparent
by the blood-letting holes in my veins;
I felt like a queen
as a captive boy
waved
at my grand entrance
from the facility's window.

Therapy

Five minute phonecall limits
shared between three payphones
and all the adult patients
at designated times.
Visitors permitted
two at a time
Tues. Fri. Sat. Sun. 6:30pm-8:30pm.
No spiral-bound notebooks.
No electronic devices,
including clocks.
No outdoor activity.
No entering another patient's room.
Not much to do here
but smoke
and eat.
Psychiatric officials find it
helps
suicidal ideation
to lock you indoors
with no reference
little stimulation
and sparse
communication.

Small Gestures

Susan is my roommate
in the mental hospital
quiet
withdrawn
with tragic medicated eyes.
I met her first
in the smoking room.
I smoked the one she offered
then returned to our room
alone
and lay in bed awake.
She silently
shuffled in and out a few times
during those hours
then walked up to my bed
and wordlessly extended her arm
above my head
dangling
another cigarette.

Brad is 19
with a monotonous
obtrusively loud voice,
every word uttered
over someone else's.
He is an institution-addicted
know-it-all
with awkward social skills
who spread
a warm blanket
over Paula,
our newest
mute

depressed
arrival,
who was lying
face down
on a couch,
dissociated
and shivering.

Ellis has a cataract
in one eye.
He only talks
to himself,
likes to count things
under his breath,
wanders the halls,
and crawls under tables.
As I was
crying
on the payphone
to my mother,
his dark hand
reached down
and placed a green pear
beside me.

White

She was in her late sixties
skin as pale as her white hair,
her arms
wrists
hands
were wrapped in a new white bandage
every morning group meeting.
When asked what her goal was for the day
she always gave the same answer,
her lips barely moving
eyes barely open
completely still
she answered almost inaudibly
"to not cut myself."

During visiting hours
her husband
would sit next to her
look to find a patch
of unbandaged skin
rest his hand there
stare straight ahead
and share her silence.

Franklin

An old patient
leans against walls
and rubs his
dick
every time I look
anywhere near him.
My first night in house,
he was sitting in the TV room
crying
over an orange
repeatedly uttering,
"I love you too, Franklin.
I don't want to eat you"
with his mouth full.

Vernon

His socks never matched
he wore a hat
layers of shirts
but carried
his pants,
his flamboyant
boxers
a beacon
as he walked in
then straight through rooms
during the middle
of group meetings.
His second day
I realized
he wore no pants
because they fell off
his emaciated waist.
Belts and strings were not allowed.
He was placed in the QUIET ROOM,
covered it with
feces
and vomit,
the clinicians
unsure
if it was intentional.
His wandering presence
absent
during group that day,
he was
cowering
in the middle of a hallway
being tied
into two hospital gowns,

weeping.
There is something
different
about
a man's
tears.

Aaron

Drug-addicted Aaron
is apprehensive
headed home
from treatment
today,
dark circles under his eyes
dark circles covering his forearm—
old cigarette burns.
I want to reassure him.
I want to kiss
his scars.

Nichole

She was boyish
with bushy dark hair
and deep-set eyes.
She wore too-big sweats
with laceless workboots.
A patient released last week,
she relapsed
and returned.
She spoke of her addictions readily—
a laundry list
containing every drug
I could fathom.
Turned to prostitution,
kicked out of missions,
sexually abused
by her father
and grandfather
from the age of 4,
they were all she had left.
"I want to be near
the love
of family,"
she asserted.
Here,
they tell us to have
a plan
in place
before we leave.

Reinvention

I will wake
each morning
with a riotous scream-song.
I will touch
others' cheeks
with soft hands.
I will switch
to thick cigars
and suck on sex.
I will eat nothing
but dripping fruit.
I will brew exotic teas
and feel hot spices
roll down my throat.
I will toast with my teacup.
I will grind
my ribs
into a fine powder
and coat
the bottoms
of my calloused feet.
I will realize
my blood
is wine.

Scars

She pulls her sleeves down
over scars.
She has vaguely mentioned
scrubbing the black
off spoon bottoms,
boys that gave it to her
if she gave herself,
shoving supermarket apples
in her pockets
to survive,
or how it starts
with a quarter bag
and escalates
to four.
I look at her—
clean
coltish
bright,
feeding her daughter
at the highchair
from a newly polished spoon.

Father

I'm glad you called.
It's been a while.
You still have the same phone number?
I'm just gonna have some people over today;
watch some football.
Trying to get my kitchen cleaned up.
How's your brother?
I'm having money struggles as usual,
but I'm still here.
I like it when you call me.
I'll try to see you real soon.
I know I'll see you Christmas,
somehow.
I better get going,
gotta get everything ready.
I love you a lot.
I can hear
the clink of his
whiskey glass
as I hang up
and set down
my wine.

Brother

Small man
tight jaw
rough grease-stained mechanics hands;
he is happiest
when getting dirty,
ripping something apart
to find a better way to put it back together.
In the car,
on the way to a family dinner
his eyes filled with tears
his calloused hands
cradling his forehead,
he shields his wet face
from others in the car;
his lover
is heartbroken
gone
after miscarrying
their first three children.

The Condom Broke

The condom broke.
We opted
for Plan B.
Later that week
in the laundromat bathroom
I found blood
in my underwear.
On our way home
we found a tiny bird
dead
too young to have even formed feathers.
We stopped
and silently
mourned.

Acceptance

I

My grandmother is dying;
my shoulders
are keeping my mother
steady,
her tears rolling down
my naked arm.

II

We sit
in warm humid air,
a glass door
away
from vibrant petals
long-rooted green
and thick damp soil.
My grandfather stands
and disappears
into the long
greenhouse,
leaving countless books of
funeral arrangements
open on the table.
"It's big,"
he says
when he returns.

III

She is gently laid down
and arranged
in bed,
legs straight,
arms light
across her chest.
He sits
on the edge,
leans over her
and tenderly kisses
her forehead.
She slowly raises
an emaciated hand
and rubs his belly.

IV

He is cleaning
out the refrigerator,
giving away
all the things
she liked to eat.
We gather
around the table,
hands on our coffee cups,
compliment the endless pastries
her sister has been baking,
look through old photographs,
play with the cat and dog,
talk about how helpful

hospice
has been.
He stands
and walks to her bed.
Her mouth
is agape
between two
yellow
bloated cheeks.
He drops more
morphine
under her tongue.

V

The corner
is empty
of her bed.
There are phone calls
fees
and visitation times.
We sit
around the table
occasionally catching
each other's eyes
attempting
empathetic smiles
through our tears.
My mother reads
the obituary
to her father.
He
weeps.

New Lovers

I

I had to sneak drinks
in the club's toilet stall;
he found me after
and offered
a sip of his,
said he had hoped
that we would
meet.
I blushed,
put my lips
to his advantageous
intentions
and swallowed

II

Kneeling
on the hardwood floor,
the clinic's number blurred
as the phonebook slid
from my knees.
I planted my hands—
cold ground an axis
to primal rocking
and cavernous
scraping
silent moans

III

The doctor leered
through piss-yellow light
and my dead-fleshed
stirrup-spread
thighs.
she pinched and tore
then withdrew
her latex fingers,
"Do you know
who gave it to you?"
I gagged
on futile words

IV

I offer
a marred
reverence wilted screaming
remembrance
seeping
forgotten petals
between clenched thigh
meat

V

Five years
of chewed youth
expectant silence
infected sex
yielded
his voice on the line
asking for forgiveness—

Step 9 of 12—
my acceptance
our reclamation

VI

I want to eat a bloody steak
with no utensils
in nothing
but my shoes.
I want to write haikus
on my palms
and sweat.
I will
smear
inhibition

First Leaves

I am freshly showered
wrapped in a towel
sitting in front of my open window in mid-afternoon.
My neighbor,
a middle-aged Native American man
walks into my yard
cradling a crying baby.
He slowly paces with her
across the green grass.
She begins to quiet
as the first red leaves of autumn
fall softly
down around them.

That First Night
for Rob Beckwith

Remember
that first night?
We sat above the river
our swinging legs
sliced through
the cool black air.
You accidentally
broke
the bottle of wine.
We opted for whiskey
and listened to old records
in your bare apartment
talked of poetry
painting
possibilities.

You moved
away
to leave them
endless.

19

You look so young
when you smoke cigars
drinking the wine
I buy.

I'm always covered
in white feathers
when I leave your bed.

Stone Fruit

My cunt
is a stone fruit
halved
honey drizzled in its recess
my lover
licks and sucks it
until slippery juice
drenches
his lips and chin
then pulls away
to rise and kiss my mouth—
the first thing
we eat
in the morning

Peace

Cradling me
he whispers kisses
over my closed eyelids
slowly
softly
strokes my breasts
with lavender sprigs

About This Moment

As we were lying in bed
after making love,
our quick breaths
the only sound
in the dark room,
red curtains open to street lamps
illuminating
the contours
of our naked bodies,
fingers
tracing
each other's hot skin,
you asked,
"Can you write something
about
this moment?"

Transcendence
for Curt Jordan

We lay in your bed
without pants
sharing
a spit-wet
beat up cigar
listening
to Kerouac's words
by candlelight
laughing over wax
accidentally spilled
hot
on my naked thigh.
We camped on the beach
in a mild Michigan January.
Sucked on chocolate.
Dreamed of mountains.
Swilled wine
while sitting back-to-back
in a dark graveyard.
Crashed on dilapidated
curb couches.
Walked at night—
you knocked on a stranger's door
for me
to ask for
this pen
and piece of paper.

Second Set: New Pictures

4 am Berrigan Marathon

Curt Jordan's Mother:
You are my Jesus clock.

Curt Jordan:
You are my upward-facing dog.

Me:
There is yoga in my panties.

Sue Cope:
You are an insightful fruit-pork maker.

David Cope:
You are a snowy kayak-lender.

Laura Meyers:
You are a weeping-haired chocolate-giver.

Keli Masten:
You are amaretto sour-soaked, pot-smoked Barbie.

John Sorensen:
You are the last olive in an NYC martini.

Mom:
You do a tiny immaculate air guitar.

Dad:
You are a whiskey-addled phone…sometimes.

Keira Edes
Your breast-to-waist ratio inspires thank-yous.

Me Again:
My poetic muscle is located in my ass.

Papa Steve:
Thank you for always buying the toilet paper.

—Melissa Wray and Curt Jordan
4-7-2007

Manhattan April 5, 2007

Sitting in a standstill cab

Hearing fruitless horns

Watching business men inhale hotdogs

on sidewalks suffocated at all hours

a different language at every crosswalk.

Laughing at women grabbing Naked Cowboy ass

Riding the subway for kicks

Imagining bucket drums

Soaking in orgasmic museum-hanged Pollock

Searching for Berrigan

Craving red fruit-stand apples

Sipping 75 cent street vendor coffee

Swooning over Monster Sushi

Eating the city raw on an empty belly

Writing without looking at the page

Elegance

My stockings
ripped near the crotch
$19 dress
even cheaper shoes
I drink a $30
glass of wine
at the NYC Four Seasons.
In the immaculate bathroom
knees and Gucci shoes
visible beneath a stall door—
a woman
gagging on her fingers
puking up her dinner.

Home!

After hitchhiking
across Vashon Island,
its hills painted
with bright lakefront homes
rising
above gray late winter water,
we sat and waited
for a ferry
to take us back to Seattle,
breathing in cool air
scented with dry wood campfires,
drinking
smuggled wine
out of disposable coffee cups.
"Apple pie and ice cream!"
you declared,
raising your cup,
spirit
pouring
through Sal Paradise eyes.

Sitting on driftwood

near an edge of Puget Sound,
both our travel bags
resting in the sand near my feet,
I watched you
bend down,
bare feet
naked ankles,
to pick through water-washed stones
and shell pieces.
I closed my eyes,
etching your image,
immersed
in the sound of waves.

Sea-Tac Airport Family Restroom

We attempt
to exit
incognito,
suppressing
our glow,
does anyone
know
we just fucked?

New Pictures

I saw a love
for you
in her eyes
that I understood.
I closed my own,
lifted
my swollen face,
allowed sunlight
to beckon
childhood freckles.

Mack

After you died
I dreamed
I had only palms.
I stared
at stubs healed over,
eyes widening
as my phantom fingers did.
I remember you,
towering Alaskan,
poppy-orange red hair,
playing basketball in the chunky boots
you showed up in—
all us addicts
herded outdoors,
faces rosying
in a rare
bright
PNW Nov. day.
I remember you
where water rivulets
crack ice,
and wonder
how much
of your
barefoot
body
was blue
when they dragged it
from the river.

1/26/16

Half Hard

My room
smelled like
his spring-worn woolen socks,
his neck
like singed
stripped cedar.
He exhaled
cheap hops and cigarettes
as we
gave our traipsing minds
mouths,
his belly
full on flowers,
he fed me
a violet.

3/20/16

For Jim and Isabella

Tiny bare limbs
nipples
round belly
she ran toward the porch
to her father
looked up at him
with playful blue eyes
which echoed his.
She tugged his hand,
he easily swung her up to his chest
her arms and legs clasping him,
they ran through the sprinkler
water spraying her little naked body
and his linen shirt and jeans,
both giggling wildly.

He approached

politely,
"Excuse me, ma'am,"
in a high
raspy voice
whistling
through his few
remaining
yellowed teeth.
"I'm trying
to catch the bus.
Just need
sixty cents
to catch the bus."
I retrieved my wallet.
He opened thick
short-fingered hands,
fingernails long
and painted black.
I gave him seventy-five.
"Just need
to catch the bus."

Traveler

A shaggy-haired man
in a dingy brown coat
with a ruddy face
and whisker-hidden mouth
is sitting on the bus seat,
a plastic bag
stuffed full
of bottles
next to him.
He lifts his leg
to cross it,
wearing
clean
new
shoes.

Medicine

The bus violently bounces
turning a sharp right
on a rickety
red brick
pothole laden street.
An elderly couple,
the wife
wearing burgundy lipstick
matching her long coat
and wool hat
is hunched in her seat
next to her husband.
Clutching his cane,
his glasses sliding down his nose,
he droopily
grumbles
"That'll shake
yer medicine up."

Blocked

With eyes
looking past me
he tells me
to write every day
about mundane things.
Smoke leaks
from his tight lips
as he pauses,
looks down,
grinds out his light
and says
he doesn't write
anymore.

Waiting

A mother
and daughter
sit
in the waiting room.
The daughter
is pensive
tired
looks like she's used to
all this.
Her mother
is next to her,
head leaned
against the wall,
face matching
her gray hair
except
for the purple
around her eyes.
She is called in.
Her daughter rises
hardened—
mother
too drunk
to stand.

Hang Woman

A display
of bones
the only thing
solid
in my starving grief,
yet some days
I eat
until pain,
cup
my belly
distended
as if with
the children
I will never
bear
you.

I had a dream
I was losing you
to happiness.
I hang
on its truth.

Contradiction

I

We wrote to each other
long-distance
for months—
a battle of wits
with undertones
of attraction.
Finally,
you were in town
and wanted to see me.
I had been
burning
for those words.

II

You took me
to an old-fashioned ice cream and candy shop.
We both
sucked on our sweets
while you drove to the bar.
After drinks
and tracing the lines
on each other's palms,
our bodies slowly moving
closer together,
you drove me home.
I hugged you over the car console.
You wouldn't let go.
You kissed me
so forcefully

that my head bent back.
You bit into
my exposed neck
and shoved your hand
down the back of my pants.
You blew a kiss
as you drove away.
I stood in the middle of my darkened street
dominated
confused
aroused
reeling.

III

In still grey
early morning light
I peeled myself
from your warm
steady-breathing
half-naked body.
As I crept to your bathroom
you lumbered into your kitchen
wild-haired
in haphazardly thrown-on clothes.
You lifted your arms languorously
and groaned.
I wondered
if I should use your toothbrush
opened your cabinet—
each product within
a small discovery.

IV

I could smell
sex
in the room
as you thrust a finger
inside me
and devoured
my breasts
with your lips and tongue.
You reached for a condom
and slowly kissed me
as you unrolled it
onto your cock.
Choking down
my desire
I said
"I can't."
You acquiesced
without hesitation,
yet still asked me
"Why?"
I told you
of the contradiction
of disease—
lust
v.
heart,
cunt
v.
conscience.
You let me cry out
my frustration
then left the bed
to wash your hands.

V

My hands
lips
tongue
enclosed you.
You moaned
reached down
groping for me
then tensed
before you released
so sweetly.
I swallowed
that emotion—
your ends
my
means.

VI

I was black-out drunk that night.
I woke the next morning
to your condescending messages
groveled my way through
your defiant
silence
angry at myself
grateful
for my
release.

Summer's coming

Days reaching humid 80
in not quite June;
I'm waiting for July—
inescapable wet heat,
its intensity undesired
except for others'
hot skin,
uncovered
exuding moist
animal spice,
accepted
without apology.

Come

My hand moved
down belly
hips
to a memory—
your voice likening
the sliding decadence
of oysters
to "tiny cunts."
My hand moved
persistent
stubborn,
body finally
sacrificing
to the thought
of giving
you
murmured
patient
pleasure.

The Fruit Is Already In Our Mouths

Reach into the crate, hesitant hand hovering for a moment over the mango's human heart shapes, until you find the one that looks "just right," curved with colors that contrast and blend simultaneously. Pick it up to test it. If it is like a woman's breast, smooth, its weight misleading for its size, move to the next test. Close your eyes and bring the stem end up close enough to touch your nose. If the scent is sticky-sweet and there is the tiniest bit of give from its skin to its meaty inside, take it home.

There is an art to peeling a mango. There is slowness and exposure involved. Don't disrespect it by merely cutting off the flesh in aggressive, uneven strips. Start small. Make one incision at the stem end, just deep enough to pierce through the skin. Drag it down and around the bottom of the fruit, then back up to meet itself. Start again at the stem, move over to the other, uncut, side and repeat. You will leave two lines circling through its thick skin, barely touching the meat.

Choose a side. Use one hand to softly sink your fingernails into the place where the two cuts meet. Sink in a little deeper and lift, loosening skin from meat. Firmly hold the tip between your fingers. Slowly pull down toward the stem. There will be a soft tearing feeling, a moist sound. If you are patient and deliberate, the diamond-shaped piece of skin will remain whole even once removed. The meat underneath will not have a perfect smoothness, as it would have had you cut the skin off haphazardly. It will look a little torn. It will feel wet and granular. The smell will be raw and incredible. Your hands will become wetter and wetter as you continue to peel away the skin from all corners. The mango may slip from your hands entirely, its juice dripping down to your wrists, permeating the cutting surface.

Don't wash the juice away so that you can manipulate the fruit more easily. Don't be afraid to lick your fingers. Wipe your palms on your upper arms. Delve back in, more aware now that you have to respect its slippery qualities. Slide it whole, in and out of your hands, then cut the meat into smaller pieces, to taste again later.

The mango's hard pit will be left behind, encased in meat that couldn't quite be cut away. You can experience it, too. Bring it to your mouth. Circle a corner with your lips, and suck. The flesh will be so compliant that it may melt off without any urging from your teeth.

These seem to be the sweetest parts.

Third Set: Iris

Vivaldi

I remember sheet music,
phonetically learning the words—
my mother remembering
her first tongue
in Sicily's musical conversation
but not in black and white.

I remember weekly visits
to my great-grandmother's house
after Sunday mass,
her floor-length silver hair
braided and twisted
into a thick bun at the nape of her neck,
a large yellow bowl
full of candy
pulled from atop the refrigerator,
lowered to my brother and me,
my mother receiving a smack
after feigning protest,
followed by
"Mangia! Mangia!"
in our direction.

I remember my grandfather
kneeling
on his faded linoleum kitchen floor
over an aluminum bowl,
both forearms
mixing bright yellow yolk
into pounds of flour
the Russo women gathered
to fill the finished dough
with fig, almond, chocolate
before twisting it
into knots,
the tradition
a struggle to uphold
after his death.

I remember hot lights
static air
slashed
by thunderous piano,
"Piango Gemo"
pouring
from my gut
like
"I love you."

Iris

I have surrendered
to finding
my strength
in vulnerability
like watching
an iris's color
intensify
with tears
or the visibility
of a bird's nest
clear
in a dying tree.

Cocksure

Dense
black
summer nights,
two barefoot
sweaty-necked
girls
perched
at porch's ledge
called out
to passing men,
gin mouths
cocksure
on prospective danger

Life Drawing

I am
stripped.
I am
shape
lines
light
absence.

Old Leather Made New

Familiar
raw
animal scent,
this slightly polished
stripped skin's
rough shine
has been attributed
by many hands—
we hold
our hides
in
each other's.

Haiku

My hair grew curly
when you moved to the mountains
I will cut it short

Heavy
for George Floyd

Spring rain
raged
overnight,
soaked blossoms
bowed
morning branches
heavy with survival.
                    6/2/20

Repose

Hold me
slow
still
by the throat,
my breastplate
brandished
for your cheek.

Sanctuary

A hip
rising to meet
lips—
the body recalls
what the heart
confines.

Upon Finding Dead Birds

Poised beak
smooth throat
no song.
Forever
mid-grasp —
celebrate
wholeness
within
our slow decay.

Softening

My skin a damp fire,
mirrored breasts
slowly teardropping,
undesired
softening
in low belly,
silver strands
in my black hair
a change as stark
and ready
as lines settling
into smile.

Our Blood

She spoke of
her previous year
as smelling sour
like something used past its date
and her mother
now staying with her from Beijing.

She unearthed
my father
the marine scent of fish
gutted over spread newspaper
and my grandfather's
bubbling marinara.

She said she now smelled of beef
wafting hands to nose
as if over a stovetop,
memories
warming our blood.

Red

With our hips crushed together
your fingers
traced surprise red,
our acceptance
cradled my uterus,
your base
slick with my blood.

Evaporate

You crouch naked
immodest
at darkened bedside
pulling on sleep pants,
soft balls hanging
under tight compact ass,
evaporating
my time-instilled
complacency.

Dry

I had a dream
we were lovers
our mouths
together
wet my eyelashes
wet between my thighs—
places I had accepted
dry.

You cannot see
an animal's tears
yet still know
its grieving.

Pour

Your words pour
as easily
as your constant cups
of smoky tea,
your eyes well
as quickly and often
when your heart
ties your tongue.

Benediction

Amidst cold
isolated
early nightfalls
atop frozen
branches,
birds sing
benediction.

www.ingramcontent.com/pod-product-compliance
Lightning Source LLC
Chambersburg PA
CBHW071212120626
46546CB00006B/2522